The Message in a Seed

GUIDELINES FOR PEACEFUL LIVING

Text by Dena Merriam

Translation of Foreword: Alice Cunningham
Design: Emily Owen, Ruder Finn Print

First published by Shumei International Press
in 2007 by Ruder Finn Press, Inc.
301 East Fifty-Seventh Street
New York, NY 10022

Printed by Ruder Finn Lithography
A division of Ruder Finn, Inc.

Printed on 100% recycled, FSC-certified paper

ISBN 978-4-903930-00-8

Printed in the United States of America

TABLE OF CONTENTS

Foreword

The extent of the environmental destruction of the earth, brought about by conventional agricultural methods, is immeasurable. Immediate conversion to sustainable agriculture is necessary. But in reality, only a very small number of farmers are converting to more sustainable farming, while most continue as before, destroying the environment. Urgent agricultural reform is hoped for as we enter what has been described as the Agricultural Century. In this environment, Shumei International is calling on not only farmers but also the public to help achieve this agricultural reform.

This book is written by Ms. Dena Merriam. After numerous trips to Japan to visit Shumei Natural Agriculture farmers throughout the country, her understanding of Shumei Natural Agriculture philosophy deepened substantially. Thus, we decided to ask her to compile a book, listing the fundamentals of Shumei Natural Agriculture from the viewpoint of an urban consumer. We hope to develop public interest in and cultivate a deeper understanding of agriculture.

Though the title of this book is *The Message in a Seed*, the purpose of the book is not to explain about the seed in detail. Agriculture begins with the act of sowing seeds in the ground. Then the soil will nurture the seed into a plant until its maturity for the harvest. This is the natural process. However, in modern agriculture, the integrity of the seed is ignored and it is looked upon simply as a tool for agribusiness. One who controls the seed will control the future of agriculture. As symbolized by the creation of genetically modified (GM) seeds, this is the corporate strategy we often see today. The primary focus of this book is the respect for nature, which Ms Merriam believes is the fundamental principle of agriculture.

In many countries, especially G8 member countries, the agricultural population is decreasing sharply, and farmers are running farms with many restraints due to various circumstances. The agricultural population in the United States is approximately 2 percent, and many farmers are being swayed by the needs of consumers and distributors. Even if we could force all farmers to convert to sustainable agriculture, they would confront great difficulties. We can't expect results from agricultural reform unless we raise the consciousness of consumers to help them deepen their understanding of agriculture. Only when we are able to shift the consumer's lifestyle toward a more sustainable one, with respect for nature, we will be able to overcome this difficulty.

How can we encourage more public interest in agriculture? Ms. Merriam lives in New York City, a densely populated urban community—I believe her understanding of Shumei Natural Agriculture can be shared with, and appeal to, the general public, most of whom have no connection with agriculture. At the same time, Ms. Merriam will introduce the concept of agriculture, food and spirituality as being an integral part of one another. This concept is the key element of the philosophy of Shumei Natural Agriculture. The superb translating abilities of Ms. Alice Cunningham, who accompanied Ms. Merriam on her visits to Japan, made it possible for her to understand the concept of Shumei Natural Agriculture in depth. Ms. Cunningham's contribution allowed us to discuss Shumei Natural Agriculture on a spiritual as well as an intellectual level while touring the farms together.

I rejoice in the publication of this book, and believe it will herald a change in people's consciousness about agriculture, nature, and spirituality, and reverse the trend of farmers moving to urban areas. Perhaps we will see a movement from the city to the farm in the future.

Koichi Deguchi, Co-Director
Natural Agriculture, Shumei International

Introduction

*I*t may seem odd to connect the way we grow our food to our ability to create a peaceful world. There has been much discussion in recent years about how our mental attitude affects the people in our environment, and in fact all the living things that we come in contact with. Each of us in our daily life has some direct bearing on whether or not we are able to live peacefully as a human community. And while the way we behave toward one another, whether we get angry, use harsh words or resort to worse, may more clearly have an impact on the level of violence in our world, so too does the way we treat our natural environment. It is not just the larger acts of violence against the environment—the destruction of forests, the dumping of toxins in oceans, the pollution of air—that affects our state of being. The less noticeable infractions have an equally critical impact— for example, the use of agricultural chemicals in our soil.

In the last few decades the amount of chemicals infiltrating our environment has soared. Today there are approximately 700,000 different chemicals in our air, water, and soil, many of which have not been proven safe. Those of us who use chemicals in our gardens and on our lawns have some responsibility to bear. The industrial production of food accounts for a large source of pollutants in the environment. It is time to ask whether it is worth the risk. With some scientists confirming the dangers posed by this chemical influx, many people are now questioning the direction we need to take in the production of food. It may also be time to explore the relationship between the way the human community treats the environment and the way we treat each other. Could disrespect and disregard in one area carry over into the other? The simple and ancient act of producing food, on which we all depend for life, may be a guide for renewing our trust in nature, and each other.

The seed is a symbol of food and nourishment. Life begins there. A starting point may be to look anew at the natural functions of the seed. The seed contains within itself all the genetic coding needed to grow into crops that nourish and sustain us. A seed contains within itself the life force that enables it to grow into food that will in turn strengthen our life energy. Within its blueprint are the nutrients required for our cells to thrive.

Some traditional cultures have retained seeds that have passed from generation to generation, and there are still some seeds today that are the offspring of crops dating back thousands of years. They have fed the human community for millennia, with very little intervention from people. These seeds from old stock are a fast-diminishing lot, as new laboratory-created seeds are beginning to rule America's fields. These newly created seeds used for the commercial production of food are no longer natural. They have been genetically manipulated to withstand insect infestation and other adversities. Most Americans don't even know which of their foods come from genetically modified seeds. These seeds have entered our food supply without significant testing for their long-term impact on human health.

As natural seeds become an endangered species, we must seek to understand the implications of this for our food supply. Each one of us will be affected. Can the disappearance of natural seeds lead to the type of food production that will be most conducive to a peaceful and sustainable world? Or does the destruction of yet another natural resource bode ill for the future health of our planet?

Those seeking to grow and consume healthy food know that a first step is to establish a relationship with the earth. And they also know that food is more than a commodity purchased in the supermarket to suit the likes and desires of the moment, or those fostered by advertisers. Food is a vital source of life sustenance, necessary for the health of body, mind and spirit. The purity of our food is essential to our overall well-being and must be protected.

Most consumers have no opportunity to engage directly in the growing of their food and leave this matter to commercial food producers, with few questions asked. Many do not even make the connection between their health, the food they eat, and the manner in which it is grown. In recent years the rise in obesity, heart problems, cancer, diabetes and other diseases has caused people to question the types of food they consume, and more and more people are now cutting down on fats and are taking other steps to modify their diets. But this concern has not yet challenged the way the agricultural industry produces our food. If we are to seriously address health concerns then we must go to the source, to the way our food is produced—looking at the conditions of the seeds and soil, and to the excessive use of chemicals.

The use of chemicals in the production of food should be a matter of concern not only to farmers but also to consumers. Since many aspects of our agricultural system directly affect our health and the health of our environment, each of us must make decisions about the type of food production we want to promote, and the quality of the food we want to ingest.

It may be difficult to see a relationship between the way we grow food and

treat the soil, and the way human beings live among each other. But if we take as a premise the interconnection of all life, knowing what we now know about how the ecosystems throughout the world affect each other, it is not a far cry to see that the way we treat nature will also affect the way we treat each other. If we approach the environment with a controlling and disrespectful attitude, we will treat other cultures and societies as well as members of our own community in the same way. We can learn the basic values of peaceful living by starting with our own garden. If we, as a community, truly practice respect for nature, this attitude will carry over into so many aspects of the life of our community, on a local, national and international level. It is a common adage that peace begins at home, with oneself and one's family. It also begins in one's own backyard garden, with the attitude we bring to the living things that surround us. There is a connection between the simple acts of growing and consuming food and the larger global problem of cultivating a more peaceful world.

Food can nourish or harm our body. Highly processed foods can damage our body, depleting it of vital resources, while naturally grown fresh foods replenish our living cells. What makes some foods beneficial and others detrimental? What have we lost and gained as our food has become mass-produced, having less and less in common with the food eaten by our ancestors? It is up to the consumer to make the effort to ensure the quality of food today, and to create a more conscious relationship with food, cultivating awareness of what goes into the growing of food so that we may develop a more healthy and sustainable lifestyle for ourselves, our family and our community.

Long before the term "globalization" came into use to describe the world's political and economic connectedness, nature was the prime example of this concept. Ecosystems, while existing in a local context, are global in their interactions and impact. Wind, water and air move freely around the globe and cannot be contained. An environmental disaster in one part of the world leaves no part untouched. The environment is truly global. Today we are struggling to understand the social and political effects of a global world economy, but nature has much to teach us. It can help us understand the interconnectedness of all things and how these interrelationships work.

Ancient peoples, like animals, were much more in tune with nature. When earthquakes or tsunamis were imminent, they knew in advance to flee. They could sense the changes within nature. Even today, animals have this premonition.

The human being, the most intelligent of Earth's creatures, having made great scientific and technological advancements, has lost the ability to understand and work in cooperation with nature. That effort begins with understanding the basic elements around us—the soil, sunlight, air and water—and how they, in their purest form, can sustain us with health and longevity.

Everything we put into the soil is carried somewhere else, and ultimately ends up in our bodies. Pesticides, herbicides and fertilizers that have been sprayed for decades onto farmland and used in backyards, gardens, on the grass and trees, as a modern convenience, a quick fix to keep away the insects and unwanted weeds, have seeped into the underground waters, into rivers and the oceans. Scientists have now identified "dead zones" in oceans around the world, due in part to seepage from these chemicals. No life grows in these dead zones – no fish, no plant life – a stark reminder of the ill effects of chemicals on the environment. And yet we are taught that there is no way to grow food successfully without chemicals. For millennia, agriculture existed without the use of chemicals. Societies flourished without modern techniques of farming. What have we gained and what have we lost?

Shumei Natural Agriculture was developed in response to these challenges. It fosters not just a natural way of growing food, but a way of living that is based on a deep and overriding respect for nature. It teaches a lifestyle that supports the health of the whole person—physical, mental, emotional and spiritual— and seeks to cultivate attitudes and actions that create a more peaceful way of being. By developing a way of life in harmony with nature, it seeks to show that the material and spiritual aspects of life are but two sides of a coin—equally necessary for the progress and advancement of our world. Agriculture brings material benefit. It also brings spiritual benefit. Shumei Natural Agriculture seeks to show how these two aspects of food production are connected and why we must now bring them together in a unified approach to living. Shumei's long-term vision is to help transform this earth into a world of beauty and harmony, without conflict and disease. To achieve this, we must re-examine our relationship to nature, to the people and living things around us, to see how we can bring harmony and beauty back to those relationships. And the starting point is the seed—the simple yet complex nature of a seed.

Chapter One

MODERN AGRICULTURE AND THE CONSUMER

*M*odern farming has created very unnatural environments in which to grow crops. It has created monocrop landscapes, in which only one crop is grown, leaving the fields devoid of natural plant and insect life. Modern farming has created farm management systems that give priority to economic activity, which depend on the growing of one cash crop at the expense of the health and well-being of the crops, the people who consume them and the environment.

This change in food production meant the advent of corporate farms—large, centrally owned crop production facilities that put many small farmers out of business. These corporate farms undertook the use of massive pesticide spraying and the intensive use of chemical fertilizers. Often these came to the market before adequate testing, and some had to be subsequently pulled and banned. They were then distributed to the developing world, where information about their health impact was not released.

The shift to mass production brought changes in consumer habits. Due to the chemical treatment of fruits and vegetables, including waxing, such foods as apples and tomatoes were now shiny and blemish free. These were presented as superior fruits and vegetables. Consumers were led to sacrifice the more healthful production of food for the perfect appearance. Along with these changes came a year-round supply of most fruits and vegetables. The concept of "being in season" was discarded and consumers in colder climates could have tropical fruits any time of year. We stopped listening to the centuries-old wisdom of the body—and listened instead to advertisers and marketers, to what they told us we wanted.

For the average consumer, the awareness of food starts in the supermarket. Walking down the aisles of today's mega-markets, the consumer thinks only of what the family wants for dinner, without considering what went into the food stacked on the shelves, or what would be most nourishing. Consumers have gotten so accustomed to the artificial appearance of many foods in the supermarket today that they do not realize how far we have deviated from the natural processes. Today's conventionally grown tomato is an ideal example.

As consumers, we have developed a lifestyle that encourages us to eat any food we want at any time of year. This may not be to our best advantage. Long-distance shipping depletes many food nutrients, and so while we may want a red tomato in the middle of the winter, if it is not locally grown, it will not provide as much nutrition as we might think.

Having the full range of vegetables and fruits available year round has made us forget what our bodies need during certain seasons. Is this really consumer demand, or the inadvertent response to food producers and advertisers, who encourage us to follow our whims rather than the real needs of our body?

Nature has created different foods during the various growing seasons, because this is what the body requires to keep itself strong and healthy during these times of year, based on climate and level of activity. One who compares the taste of the supermarket tomato bought in the dead of winter to the taste of a freshly picked tomato during its proper growing season, raised without chemicals, can easily discern the difference. Tomatoes from the field are sweet and satisfying, with a rich full flavor that tells something of their inherent nutritional value. Out-of-season tomatoes have little or no taste.

What we have lost as we have advanced technologically is our ability to listen to and understand nature, which for millennia has been the farmer's best guide on all matters. This is the wisdom we must recapture, but it is now up to every consumer, not just the farmers, to gain this understanding, because it is market demand that will ultimately direct the farmer to the type of food to grow.

Contemporary society is based upon the premise of a quick-fix approach to life. If you are hungry, find some fast food to fill the stomach. If you are farming and an insect appears, spray it away. If you need more crops to make a greater profit, add chemicals to the soil for an immediate increase in production. If there is drought, seed the clouds with chemicals—and so on. The common thinking seems to be—don't spend time trying to understand why nature has responded in a particular way, but rather override the natural processes by imposing a short-term fix, without considering the long-term consequences. Don't bother to understand nature. Devise an artificial solution—regardless of the ultimate result. Our society has failed to think through how our reckless behavior toward the environment will boomerang. We are introducing genetically modified foods without adequate research into the long-term impact on our health and the environment. We cannot leave such decisions to corporate interests or policymakers. Our health and well-being are at stake.

We have reached a critical point where the public must regain control, to the degree that it can, over the factors that affect health. The public is beginning to understand the need to speak out and change food-purchasing and eating habits. Just as some years ago, knowledge about the relationship of exercise to health began to awaken, and yoga, jogging and other forms of exercise began to flourish, so there is a growing understanding of the relationship between what we eat and our health. An indication of this awareness is a rise in the consumption of natural and organic foods.

Recognition is also growing of the deep environmental crisis we face. While there is much discussion of climate change, global warming, and the need for new energy sources, not enough attention has yet been paid to the impact of chemicals on the environment and our health. In fact, these issues are related.

Shumei Natural Agriculture is based on knowledge of this interrelationship. It seeks to change the way we relate to our food, and to put the growing of food back in the hands of consumers. It seeks to build a new partnership between food growers and consumers for the common goal of producing healthy food that enriches rather than depletes and harms the environment.

Chapter Two

THE BIRTH OF SHUMEI NATURAL AGRICULTURE

*I*n the early part of the 20th century, Japanese naturalist and agriculturalist Mokichi Okada (1882–1955) developed a system of food production called Natural Agriculture based on a deep respect for nature. It advocates a natural growing process without the use of any fertilizers or agricultural chemicals. Now embraced and taught by Shumei, an environmental, spiritual and cultural organization based in Japan, Shumei Natural Agriculture guides farmers to work in harmony with nature, developing in them an understanding of its laws, cycles and inherent principles. It also enables consumers to be more aware of the quality of food they eat, so they can make choices that will result in better health and well-being.

Mokichi Okada was born on December 23, 1882, in Tokyo, and grew up in extreme poverty. Born frail, he suffered from numerous diseases throughout life. The medical treatments provided by the physicians of his time had an adverse effect on him and he was left to his own resources, seeking new therapies that would improve his health. He had many difficulties in his personal life, suffering the loss of his wife and many financial burdens during the economic depression of the 1920s and 30s. As a result of his trials, Mokichi Okada turned more and more to the spiritual, seeking deeper understanding of the forces that bring harmony and balance to life. He also became a great connoisseur of the arts, and promoted the belief that beauty has the power to uplift and transform our lives. He began to see agriculture as an art, and came to believe that the relationship with soil and crops also has the power to change our lives. Thus

over time he increasingly devoted himself to cultivating crops and spreading an agricultural movement based on a harmonious way of relating to nature. During those middle years of the 20th century, pesticide and fertilizer use was becoming widespread. At that time it had nowhere near the market penetration that it has today, but there was also little opposition. Society was infatuated with science and new technologies, and the idea of multiplying food production many fold was captivating to all sectors involved in food production—farmers, transporters, marketers, advertisers, and even consumers.

Mokichi Okada saw the direction that agriculture was taking, and he set out to renew the relationship between people, soil and crops. This relationship was based on two essential concepts. First and foremost was the profound physical and spiritual connection between humankind and nature. Second was the imperative of fostering an overriding respect for nature, which comes from understanding the laws of balance, harmony and interaction.

Chapter Three

RESPECTING NATURE:
THE RELATIONSHIP BETWEEN FARMER AND NATURE

$\mathcal{F}$armers who work in harmony with nature attest to the profound changes that this relationship has brought in their lives. It has generated not only deeper understanding of the laws and principles of nature, but it has also fostered a genuine respect for elemental forces, which humans have never been able to control. Until the 20th century, when technology and science began to dominate humanity's relationship to nature, there had existed an almost reverential respect for the natural world. Poets and painters have for centuries held nature in awe. Ancient cultures had similarly understood the magnitude of the natural powers and the ways to work in harmony with them. We have slowly lost this awareness. Mokichi Okada saw the need to renew the damaged link between people and the natural world. He saw the negative impact, both on the individual and on society, of working against nature. He saw that by seeking to control nature, we were causing ourselves not only physical but also emotional, mental and spiritual harm.

Natural Agriculture fosters a way of interacting with nature that affects the whole of one's life. It is a holistic approach to cultivating food. The Natural Agriculture system is one in which the relationship to nature that develops through the growing of food will affect one's perception of the world. This movement does not separate food into an independent category of life, but rather is based on a fundamental understanding of the interconnection between our food and our overall well-being—physical, mental, emotional, social and spiritual. It takes into account our health and the health of soil, water and air, and the ecosystems of the earth. If they are healthy, we will be healthy. If they are unhealthy, this will adversely affect human well-being.

As mentioned earlier, the health of the earth will be assured only when we modify our lifestyles to be more in harmony with nature. To develop this relationship with nature, we must seek to understand the natural laws and abide by them. When we respect an individual, we don't try to control him or her, but rather to understand and act in accordance with the beliefs of that person. The same is true of our relationship with nature. For example, the farmer's decision to multiply crop production will demand the use of chemicals, but this will ultimately weaken and pollute the natural systems. This is an example of the farmer imposing his or her will on the environment. It would be far better to care for the natural yield without forcing an artificial plan or timetable on the soil, knowing that over time the crops will increase on their own.

Compared with the modern technological approach to farming, one might call this a method of non-intervention, letting nature take its own course and work in its own way. But that is a simplification of the philosophy and approach. In fact, it demands close cooperation between farmer and nature. One must be far more attentive, observing what is taking place in the soil, observing the surroundings, knowing that the proximity of trees and water, the degree of sunlight, the conditions of the air, the attitude one takes, the care of the soil, how the crops are planted, what they are surrounded by, and numerous other factors all have significant impact. It is not just a matter of putting a seed in the ground and watering it. One must come to care for the seed and subsequent

crop, respecting the integrity of the natural growing process, understanding the physical and spiritual linkages, and most importantly approaching the process with a true sense of gratitude. It is not we who are growing the crop. We are the guardians, the instruments. It is nature who is giving her bounty, and there is much we can do to draw out the resources, to support the internal processes that give rise to healthy crops. Mokichi Okada recognized this and set forth a philosophy of Natural Agriculture that is at its core a way of life, a total system of living that helps us become more conscious of the growing and consuming of food as a spiritual exercise, an art, a way of expressing gratitude to nature, to the Creator and to each other.

Nature is perfect in itself, and we human beings are only a part of the whole. Instead of trying to control nature, a more harmonious attitude would be to adjust ourselves to it and cultivate respect. As we begin to respect nature, we come to honor the wisdom and the ways, the beauty of its workings, knowing that if we seek to control nature we are stepping out of harmony with the natural cycles of life, which will go on and on, long after we are gone from this earth. As we recapture a relationship with nature long held by our ancestors, we come to it in a new light, now knowing the damage and degradation that is wrought when we seek, with our limited understanding, to impose a "better way" on systems that have worked for millennia. The scientific knowledge we have gained must be balanced by our intuitive, creative, more artistic awareness, which knows our need for attunement with nature. It is a balance between the science and the art of growing food. Agriculture, having become a tool of technology and science,

must be reclaimed as an art, so we can regain our intuitive and profoundly replenishing relationship with the forces that are vital to our survival.

Once our attitude toward nature begins to change, and we respond to nature as a living organism, we will find that our trust in the natural forces also grows—a trust that with the proper attitude on our part, nature will respond in a positive fashion. Trust is an essential quality in our relationships with other people, and we can apply this same principle to our relationship with nature.

This approach is not to step back in time and overlook technological advances. Rather, it is to understand where technology has failed, and to draw upon our own innate resources to help retool our relationship with the growing of food. The increase in population and change in lifestyle have placed tremendous stress on our planet, and we must step back and assess in order to see how to restore our planet and sustain healthy ecosystems. For this to take place, a change in attitude is needed—an understanding of the spiritual sustenance we derive from nature. Our need for a healthy natural world can be understood as far more than material. The deeper aspects of the relationship must also be addressed.

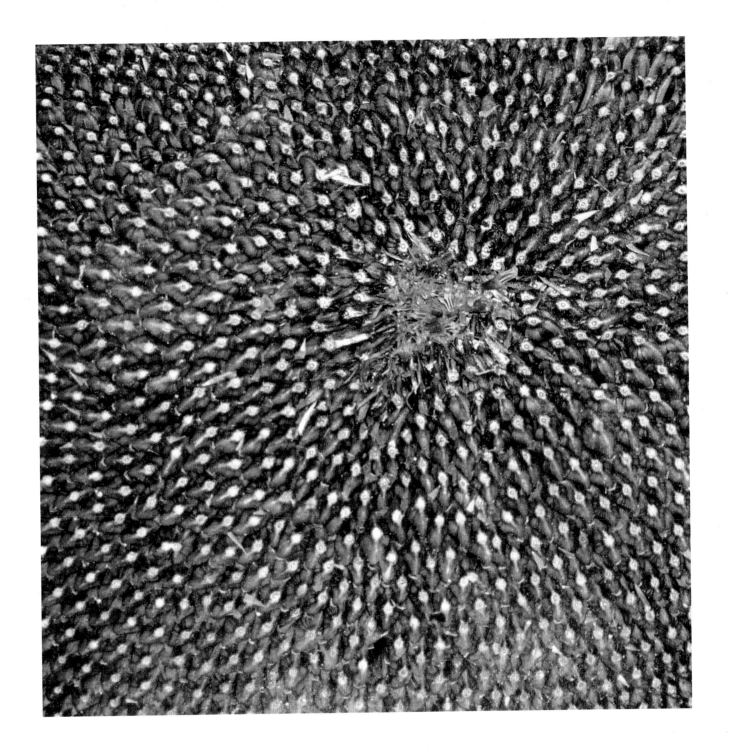

Chapter Four

Damage Caused by Agricultural Chemicals and Fertilizers

*B*illions of invisible creatures live in the soil—including bacteria. The earth is a vital living system. These creatures help enrich the soil and are needed for healthy plant life. If one were to look at soil under a high-powered microscope, one would find a great variety of microscopic life—mites, fungi and nematodes involved in various functions, composing a vast, interdependent community of life. Farmers have attested to the importance of the multitude of organisms in the soil if the land is to produce high-quality crops. There is a difference in crop taste after soil has been saturated with chemicals and the living organisms killed. The greater the diversity of organisms in the soil, the higher the quality of food.

Plants do not just absorb nutrients from the soil; they also exude carbohydrates through their roots, feeding the tens of millions of microorganisms in the soil. In its natural state, soil is pure and contains all the elements needed for healthy plant growth. The balance of life in the soil is of critical importance to the growth of healthy crops.

When agricultural chemicals are applied to the soil, they destroy this rich universe of life. When pesticides are sprayed, only the pesticide-resistant life survives; everything else dies, just as antibiotics don't distinguish between the good and the detrimental bacteria—they attack them all.

In the industrialized world, the use of chemicals has grown to enormous proportions in recent years, with no calculation of the health or environmental risks. On average, farmers in the industrialized countries use 206 kilograms (approximately 440 pounds) of fertilizer per hectare (approximately two and a half acres) of land, compared with an average of 9 kilograms of fertilizer per hectare in sub-Saharan African countries.

This, of course, creates a vicious cycle of chemical dependence. The more one uses fertilizers, even organic fertilizers, the more one weakens the soil's ability to defend itself, and the more likely it is to have an infestation of insects, thereby causing the conventional farmer to use more pesticides, generating a never-ending cycle of chemical use. The crops become weaker, leaving them vulnerable to more insect damage. In depleting the soil, the industrialized methods of farming have created a cycle that requires greater use of pesticides for the crops to grow.

Numerous trace minerals are required to produce healthy, nutrient-rich crops. Industrial farming destroys the vast majority of these. With many of the soil-based microorganisms killed by chemicals, there is no way of replenishing these trace minerals, which are needed by our bodies. They boost our immune system and help fight off disease. One of the most serious environmental challenges today is the depletion of the soil, and the subsequent low nutritional quality of our food. We do not even know all the ways in which this decrease in food quality is affecting human health.

The flooding of our environment with agricultural chemicals infiltrates not only the soil but also the water and the air, and ultimately these chemicals find their way into our cells, damaging our cellular structure and making us vulnerable to abnormal cell growth—or cancer—as well as other diseases.

Chapter Five

ALTERNATIVE WAYS OF DEALING WITH INSECTS

There are healthy methods for dealing with insects. As respect for nature grows, one begins to see the role of humans in a different light. We are not here to impose our will, but rather to see how we can support and guide. For example, if insects appear on crops, the conventional farmer will immediately use pesticides. The Natural Agriculture farmer will respond differently, picking off the larger insects but encouraging the health of the plant so that it can fight off the insects on its own. Even if the crops suffer, the Natural Agriculture farmer will know not to use pesticides because of their long-term effects. These farmers do not to think in terms of a short-term fix at the expense of human health, and the health of the soil and future plant life. When fertilizers and pesticides are used, insects become a permanent problem, because the plants don't develop the ability to fight off these pests on their own.

There is an underlying reason for the emergence of insects, and of diseases caused by bacteria. They are part of the normal cycle of nature and have a role to play. One must have patience to see the plants through difficult periods when they may not grow as well or be as productive. It is like seeing a child through a cold or virus. In time, the child recovers, if well cared for. Doctors now warn against giving children antibiotics every time they are unwell. It is now known that the overuse of antibiotics can weaken the immune system.

Similarly, plants must learn to live with insects, and the more we attend to the plants and watch their growing conditions, the more we encourage their strength and health, the more likely insects are to become only a slight annoyance. Plants and insects can coexist. As the amount of fertilizer and agricultural chemicals in the soil decreases with time, the plants will become stronger. There is a direct correlation between the decrease of fertilizers and agricultural chemicals and the decrease of insects and disease. Just as drug addicts experience symptoms of withdrawal, so too soil must experience a period of purification where it rids itself of fertilizers and agricultural chemicals. This may be a time when insects attack. One must not give in to the impulse to find an immediate solution, but rather understand that the soil and plants need time to strengthen their innate resources. The plants, which are so used to receiving fertilizers, need time to recover their natural ability to absorb nutrients from the soil instead of relying on artificial additives. The soil also needs time to recover its nutrients.

Just as a healthy person resists illness even if everyone around gets sick, so too a healthy plant will be able to withstand and coexist with insects, without suffering damage. But the plant first needs to strengthen itself. This takes time.

The key quality needed for cultivating respect for nature is patience. Grasses and plants growing in the wild don't need the help of chemical or organic fertilizers or pesticides. They manage to get all the nutrients they need, and they co-exist with insects, which do not flock to them but eat naturally their share of plant life without causing harm to the plants. We have grown so accustomed to applying chemicals to get the results we want that we have lost sight of what is natural. We must return to seeing the benefit and beauty of the natural environment.

Most often, healthy soil and healthy plants will be able to resist and coexist with insects. Of course there are exceptions, when there is an infestation of locusts or some other insect. But these times are rare, and even then, natural solutions can be applied. And it is important to seek to understand why such an imbalance has occurred. The key is to change from short-term to long-term thinking if we are to foster the health of our planet, and to care for our own health.

Chapter Six

CARING FOR SOIL NATURALLY

*U*sing the Shumei Natural Agricultural method, farmers apply to the soil only natural compost made of tree leaves and grasses. They do not utilize any fertilizers or agricultural chemicals, despite any problems that may emerge. Natural compost keeps the soil moist and stimulates the natural growing power within the earth.

Mokichi Okada taught that natural soil has all the components needed to produce healthy grains and vegetables. Indeed, the function of soil is mysterious. With all its advances, modern science still does not really understand the properties of soil and how it produces healthy crops. Soil left to its own devices is full of nutrition. It is one of the mysteries of nature, like the creation of life itself, which can never be understood by scientific knowledge alone. This does not mean that a person cannot work with the soil, helping to cultivate its inherent growing powers. But the use of fertilizers and pesticides weakens its power and disturbs its balance, destroying some essential life forms, leading to crop disease and insect damage. Soil damaged by the use of fertilizers can take years to recover its natural growing powers. When Natural Agriculture farmers take over fields used in conventional farming, the soil usually takes several years to recover. After a few years of growing food without any chemicals or unnatural additives, the soil becomes rich and full of nutrients. There may be a temporary decline in yield, but this is due to the healing process of the soil, which is seeking to rebalance and replenish itself with the microorganisms needed for life.

Because conventional farmers think of the soil as merely something to support food production, they do not realize the damage done by adding fertilizers and agricultural chemicals into the soil. We should realize that the soil responds to conditions, just as humans respond to conditions. Everything comes about through will, and thus the soil has a will to grow crops. It is its natural function. The soil has grown all kinds of living things from ancient times by its own will and power. From this perspective, the addition of chemicals or organic fertilizers reduces the independence and dignity of the soil. Nature has its own perfection.

The current state of our environment, and the process of global warming with its many unknown effects, should teach us that it is a great mistake to seek to control nature. Use of fertilizers and agricultural chemicals may bring a temporary growth in food production, however, as time goes by, we will see that the negative effects of using fertilizers are far greater than the positive aspects. This is evident when we compare the root systems of crops grown with and without the addition of chemicals. Crops grown without any additives have root systems that are stronger and far more developed. Those grown with chemicals have less-developed root systems, as they have grown dependent on chemical additives and do not gain nutrients in the same way from the soil.

Nature maintains the balance of the whole ecosystem of the earth, and this balance ultimately provides the most favorable conditions for human life and all other living things. Nature's will is inherent in the soil. So respecting the will of the soil is a primary condition for respecting nature. The breakdown of natural systems through our intervention will ultimately lead to the collapse of balance

on a much larger scale, and eventually both nature and human beings will face serious consequences.

The soil enriches itself through nitrogen, which is naturally produced as a result of heat rising up from the deeper layers of the earth. This nitrogen is the soil's own naturally produced fertilizer. It rises up through the surface of the earth and gathers above the soil, from where it is carried back down by the rain soaking into the soil. As a naturally occurring phenomenon, this natural fertilizer has all the properties required by nature to produce nutritionally rich and balanced food. When we look around at natural landscapes, such as forests, we see that nature has done a wonderful job of producing an abundance of large, healthy trees without the use of additives.

For millennia nature has done quite well on its own, without any interference from humans, supporting a rich array of life whose diversity is staggering and well beyond anything we humans could have produced. It is we who, through our lack of understanding and wisdom, are now threatening this diversity and sapping nature of its ability to flourish. And in doing so, we are sadly harming ourselves.

Chapter Seven

THE IMPORTANCE OF SELF-GROWN SEEDS

*T*he seed is the starting point in the cycle of life. When we sow a seed in the soil, nature nurtures the seed, and thus it grows. And nature will give us hundreds or even a thousand times more seeds as fruits of this act. We consume most of the harvest, and then we return a part as seeds to the land. Nature gives us bounty. We merely sow the seeds. Nature does the rest. This is how an attitude of gratitude begins. To be grateful for the fruit and for the beginnings of the next harvest is to practice the art, not the science, of agriculture.

Many cultures held the seed sacred, because it contains all the elements of life. But today seeds produce income, and thus the concept of the sacredness of seeds is disappearing. For those who promote Natural Agriculture based on respect for nature, the understanding of the seed as a sacred gift is indispensable. Those who have cultivated an attitude of gratitude understand the power of the seed, and know to sow it in the soil with their own hands to save the seed, and to express thankfulness by returning a portion of the seed to the land.

Mokichi Okada taught that as we human beings can learn from various experiences, so we can learn from seeds. He pointed out that a seed can take on the character of the soil and the climate in which it is sown. The seed has the ability to adapt and develop its faculties to adjust to the environment.

For example, when we sow soybeans from a warm climate in a cold region, they cannot grow well initially. They don't have the knowledge of the cold area, and they cannot adjust to it. Seeds react sensitively to the environment. As we save the seeds every year and plant them, they will over time adjust to the soil and the natural features of the region, and eventually they will be able to grow well in that climate. In this way, they adapt.

Unfortunately, few of today's farmers save their own seeds. We can say that it is an unnatural act to buy seeds even if they are organically grown. This is especially true of the hybrid variety and genetically modified (GM) seeds. It is part of nature's rhythm to sow seeds into the land where they were grown.

We cannot create seeds artificially. Nature will react if we modify seeds to suit human whim. To sell and buy modified seeds, eliminating naturally produced seeds, is to create serious damage, which will have long-term consequences for the security of our food system.

Genetically modified seeds are those that have had external genes implanted into their gene code. One type of genetically modified seeds does not reproduce itself. These are called terminator seeds, because the crops that they yield do not produce seeds at the end of their growing cycle. Thus, farmers using this new breed of seeds must purchase them every year from the chemical companies that produce them, taking away the farmers' ability to maintain himself or herself independently—and tampering with the cycle of life.

Because these new types of modified seeds are disease and pest resistant, they are being promoted widely. But just as bacteria and viruses adapt to circumvent antibiotics, it is only a matter of time before natural pests find ways to circumvent these new types of seeds.

There is much concern among environmentalists and organic farmers about this development in the seed industry. An effort is now under way to preserve the pure, untampered seeds that have passed from generation to generation of plant life, so that traditional crops from natural stock will not disappear. Good seeds will produce healthy and tasty crops. Engineered seeds will not produce the same quality of crops.

Seeds are a precious resource. They hold the key to life. All the elements needed for the development of crop life are contained in the seed. For millennia, people from all cultures have known to treasure and protect their seed stock. There is a reason for this. Seeds hold the life force, and their energy is transmitted to the plant and ultimately to our cells and organs. The quality of the seed is of critical importance. Hopefully, in the years ahead, our farmers will have the wisdom to preserve this vital natural asset.

Chapter Eight

THE PRODUCER-CONSUMER RELATIONSHIP

$\mathcal{U}$ntil recent times, people knew where their food was being grown, who the farmer was and how the crops were being tended. We have lost this relationship in the modern world. We now look at food as a commodity. Instead of seeing it as providing the nutrients vital to life and good health, it has become merely a quick, convenient source of energy, to keep us going while satisfying a taste or desire. The number of processed and packaged foods in the supermarket is a testament to this, as is the rise of the fast food industry.

Consumers have not considered these issues to be important. They have left the matter of growing food in the hands of the farmers. We have forgotten the relationship between the eating of food and the maintenance of life. Food is our vital link to good health, and consumers should educate themselves about this relationship. We cannot expect farmers, whose priorities are economic growth and profitability, to educate consumers. It is a task each one of us must undertake as we assume responsibility for our own well-being.

We can reeducate ourselves about the resources of nature and the principles that govern the natural cycles. We can learn again how to grow natural foods, relying only on the wisdom of nature and what it teaches us when we attune ourselves to the natural ways of growing. We can learn again to listen to our bodies and the wisdom that is built into our cellular structure. After all, we are part and parcel of nature. The same elements that exist in the soil, water and trees are also in us. We are inextricably linked, and when we harm and deplete the soil, we also harm ourselves.

Today some people are returning to the local Natural Agriculture farmer as a way of developing a relationship again with the growing of their food. They know that the personal touch directly affects the quality of the food. In communities throughout Japan with Natural Agriculture farmers, consumers have a direct relationship with these farmers and attest to the difference this has made in their understanding of the relationship between food and health. Although similar community models exist, Shumei Community Supported Agriculture has led to the development of more efficient structures. Under this arrangement, a group of consumers come together and purchase food directly from a farmer. The farmer delivers food to a central location each week, and consumers divide up the food according to what they have purchased, bypassing the need for third-party marketers. The benefit of this system is that the consumers work directly with the farmer. They know his or her farming methods and what crops are being grown. They learn to depend on the character and integrity of the farmer. The farmer, on the other hand, develops a personal commitment to the consumers, knowing that the crops will be eaten by individuals toward whom he or she feels a sense of responsibility. A very special bond is cultivated.

These relationships have led consumers who want to be more involved in the production process to help out on the farm during the harvest. This relationship can exist even in the cities, when suburban farmers bring their produce directly to consumers so that city dwellers can eat locally grown food.

In interviews with both farmers and consumers who participate in Shumei Natural Agriculture programs in Japan, it is clear that this relationship changes the attitude of farmers, and deepens the relationship of consumers to the natural cycles, despite where they live. Consumers who buy directly from farmers know what crops are grown during which season, and they understand why their body needs these food products during that seasonal cycle. They learn to eat seasonally. The Natural Agriculture farmer cannot function if he or she does not live close to the land, the soil and the elements. The farmer must be in direct contact with all of these forces, and the consumer, through the farmer, can come to know them as well. This experience changes our perception of the natural world and makes it an essential part of life. We begin to see nature as a great living organism of which we are an integral part. Once we have that understanding, we cannot consider imposing techniques that would harm any part of the whole.

Chapter Nine

THE ART OF AGRICULTURE: FINDING BEAUTY
AND GRATITUDE

*O*ur relationship with nature is a physical one. Our bodies depend on its resources. We need air, water and earth, from which food comes and on which our cells depend. But it is also a spiritual relationship, as this nourishment affects our emotional, mental and spiritual well-being. Poets and artists have long known the healing effects of beauty—particularly the beauty of nature. It uplifts the spirit and provides a deep inner fulfillment. Nature has a great healing capacity, and the growing of crops is no exception. Anyone who has worked the soil, tended crops, seen their growth and the coming of their fruit and seed knows the power of beholding this mystery of life as it unfolds. To see the seed start new life, grow into a seedling and then into a plant, and then into a crop for eating, and begin a new life cycle with seed again, is to witness a wondrous process, which should not be taken for granted. It is creation, and artistry of the highest form.

Our society speaks of agricultural technology, the science of food production, but we have forgotten the beauty and art that is an intrinsic part of agriculture. To see this is to shift the way we relate to the growing of food.

When we are in the presence of beauty there is often an accompanying experience of appreciation—a gratefulness for all that beauty brings to us, for the upliftment and comfort, the heightened sense of being. How often are we struck by the beauty of light falling upon a branch or leaf, the graceful body of a tree, the movement of grass and other plant life? There is so much about our world that can strike our senses and produce amazement, if we take the time to really see.

There is a difference between farmers who concentrate only on the technical aspects of growing food, and those who discern the beauty inherent in the process. The latter are more likely to experience appreciation and gratitude for what nature has offered.

Shumei Natural Agriculture farmers often refer to a change in awareness as they work closely with crops over a period of time. They speak about a gratitude that naturally develops, and they consider this to be an essential ingredient of their success. They understand that crops are a gift of nature, of the soil, sun and water, and they are grateful for the natural forces that enable the production of these crops. This gratitude translates into a new relationship to the crops and the environment.

Attitude is a key factor in the success of any endeavor, and agriculture is no exception. The farmer's perceptions of the environment, soil and crops will affect the quality of the yield. If a farmer cultivates an attitude of respect, understanding and gratitude will naturally follow, and the farmer will find himself or herself aligned with the laws of nature. This ultimately will bring positive results.

Like respect for nature, the concept of gratitude must be naturally acquired. It cannot be studied or taught. The feeling of gratitude toward nature is an inner experience that develops over time. It is an expression of our basic attitude toward life and the forces that sustain us. Farmers and consumers who have adopted a Natural Agriculture way of life find that as they develop gratitude toward nature, this feeling begins to permeate their whole approach to life—so they may feel greater thankfulness for their work, their family, their health, their

achievements and their gifts in life. One might say that as we deal with nature, so we deal with life. This quality of gratitude is an essential element of happiness, and thus our approach to nature is a key component of our spiritual lives.

For many people, spirituality is the means to pursue meaning, fulfillment and happiness in life. One's mental attitude is a key factor in this pursuit. The cultivation of gratitude sets one in a relationship to the world that enables one to see all the good and the benefits that naturally flow, and it establishes the positive framework in which happiness can grow. Gratitude is a key, and nature can provide us that opening, helping to nurture this positive way of thinking and being. Over time, as one develops a new relationship with plants and crops, and the natural forces that sustain them, an attitude of gratefulness blossoms of itself. This can be cultivated by carrying it into every phase of one's daily life, and little by little we will see that our material successes are being met and guided by a spirituality that is deeply rooted in natural processes.

Life is both material and spiritual. By tapping the spiritual as well as the material forces of nature, we can understand the balance that is needed. This will bring us into greater harmony and alignment with nature.

Chapter Ten

THE BALANCE BETWEEN MATERIALISM AND SPIRITUALITY

*M*odern advances have led to greater economic disparities and greater tensions between the industrialized and non-industrialized countries—leading to new forms of violence and conflict. There is a relationship between the type of development the international community is promoting—one divorced from the natural way of life—and growing world tensions. The dangers are clear if we continue our patterns of over-consumption and rapid depletion of nature's resources.

We can work to foster new attitudes. Mokichi Okada did not deny materialism. He believed in a balance of the material with the spiritual. He believed that material development should be guided by spiritual wisdom: that the development of wealth and the increase in productivity was not a bad thing, but that it must be achieved by working in harmony with the natural laws, not in opposition to them. Mokichi Okada taught that both aspects of life are necessary, that you cannot have true spiritual development without the material, and that you cannot have sustainable material development without the spiritual foundation. Materialism without spirituality is a dangerous course to pursue.

By spirituality we mean understanding the interconnectedness of life, knowing the proper role and value of nature, cultivating the caring and compassionate qualities of human nature, and sharing and putting into action our love and concern for others, and indeed all creation. Spirituality is a very real human need. One of the challenges facing people today is to find a lifestyle that balances materialism with spirituality, so that we can be in greater harmony with ourselves and the world.

Some people may regard the spiritual side of life as separate from the material, but Mokichi Okada saw them as intimately linked. Thus he saw Natural Agriculture as the effort to bring back to agriculture the spiritual knowledge of how to maintain the balances in the natural world. Natural Agriculture, as he saw it, helps the farmer regain harmony with the natural environment and to work with better understanding of nature. If we can invigorate our material culture with a spiritual culture as well, we will improve our well-being significantly.

The material perspective looks only to improve productivity, without taking care of overall well-being. A spiritual approach would take into consideration the whole range of issues, knowing that it is not wise to seek short-term gain at the expense of the long-term welfare.

Chapter Eleven

LEARNING FROM SEEDS

*W*hen the integrity of nature is damaged for personal gain, we know that we have lost understanding of our proper relationship with nature, of our interdependence. Until we make the link between the destruction committed against nature and the violence in our society, we will not be able to overcome the negative forces in our society, or in the environment. If we are committed to a peaceful world and the overcoming of violence, we must examine carefully the way our society deals with nature.

If individuals change their attitude toward nature, this will ultimately be reflected in our collective culture. These principles have great relevance to what is happening in the world today. We cannot divorce our methods of agricultural production from the tremendous disruptions in the environment, and even the conflicts among nations. To understand the nature of interconnectedness is to know that how we treat the Earth will affect all else. The mindset that seeks to dominate and impose itself on nature is one that will seek to do this to other peoples and cultures. By respecting nature, we also come to respect all others. To understand and put into practice the philosophy of Natural Agriculture is to provide benefit to the world, and help set a new paradigm that will lead to peace, sustainability and greater well-being for all.

The spread of western culture has stressed the importance of material wealth, but it has not necessarily brought an improvement in the human condition or greater human happiness. Wealth and happiness are not linked. Certain aspects of life have improved, no doubt—life expectancy is longer, we have learned to control certain diseases, technology has made life easier in many respects,

and some of us have more leisure time. On the other hand, new diseases have cropped up and our fast-paced lives have created more tension and stress. The degradation of our environment has created not only health hazards but it has also taken an emotional and spiritual toll. This degradation will be felt for generations to come, and it will lead to more serious global challenges if it is not soon addressed in a way that can slow or reverse the damage.

Peace begins with oneself. We cannot hope to stop conflict if we are prone to anger and violence in our own lives. If everyone were to learn to settle differences through nonviolent means, governments, being a collection of individuals, would eventually follow suit. This may not stop conflict altogether, but we could make much progress in aborting the violence that now plagues our societies. What can seeds teach us about living peacefully?

The growing of vegetables without chemicals and fertilizers takes patience and the cultivation of a new attitude toward nature and life. It means believing in the healing, restorative powers of nature. The farmer must learn to curb the learned reaction of reaching for the quick fix to destroy the "opponent." The farmer must learn not to impose himself or herself on the natural process. He or she must learn to see the insect not as an enemy but as a part of this vast web of nature to which we all belong. He or she must work patiently, quietly, by the side of the crop to help bolster its own innate support system so that it can outwit the insect. This takes a change in mindset. But if what we do, how we behave, has a ripple effect, touching all parts of the natural world, the spread of this attitude will affect the way we treat each other, as well as the way we treat the natural world. The more we can cultivate crops peacefully, without the

arsenal of pesticides and fertilizers, the more this attitude of respect for nature will spread and affect the way we treat our forests, our water systems, wetlands, animals, air, and so on. It will help us address the overwhelming challenge of reversing the environmental damage already incurred. We cannot leave this challenge to governments, policymakers or corporations. Too much is at stake. The responsibility falls on each one of us.

Scientists are beginning to find concrete evidence of the interconnectedness of life. A study of rats in one laboratory who were taught certain behavioral changes found that subsequently rats in other parts of the world were able to learn this trait far more quickly than the initial group. A transfer of knowledge was made. Some conclude that this is why in the ancient world, cultures separated by oceans made discoveries at the same time. There is a common thread through which all of life is linked—like a common database into which we tap. Thus a change of attitude and relationship to nature on the part of a small group of people can help shift the tide in many parts of the world, perhaps even reversing the environmental damage already done and leading to a slowing down of climate change. The way we treat the soil and plant life will affect all environmental concerns. Cultivating respect and gratitude for nature can affect consumption, waste, energy use, and a host of other issues—all of which will help determine the way communities relate to one another. If energy or water are in short supply in the years ahead, due to the disruption of the natural balance, this is likely to lead to conflict and wars, if we don't attend now to our way of relating to nature—and ultimately one another. Nature is emitting a cry of urgency. Let's hope that we hear and respond.

Conclusion

What Each One of Us Can Do

At the 101st session of the World Health Organization in 1998, the Executive Board proposed that the World Health Assembly adopt a draft revision of the "definition of health," and it was adopted. The traditional definition of health was that "Health is a state of complete physical, mental and social well-being and not merely the absence of disease or infirmity," but to this definition, the word "spiritual" was added, demonstrating that spiritual health is a key component of well-being, in addition to physical, mental and social health. Our society is beginning to recognize the link between these various aspects of human life. Translating this awareness into practical actions means changing behavior. How can we integrate this understanding into our daily lives? There are small ways to start.

The growing of food should not just be left to professional farmers. It is an activity that each and every one of us should engage in—whether one has a few pots on a city balcony or a small suburban garden, or a community garden in a vacant city lot. It is a way to strengthen our relationship with nature. If more of us were to engage in the simple act of growing food naturally, we would find a transformation not just in our own consciousness but also in the greater community. We would naturally begin to eat more healthfully and to be conscious of the impact of food on our bodies and minds. Eating healthier foods will give us a greater sense of peace and well-being. We would find ourselves more respectful and caring toward nature. The changes engendered in our lives would be visible—and no doubt, little by little, we would see the emergence of a

more peaceful, less violent society. There are many ways to work toward world peace—by helping to relieve poverty, through education and employment, and by working for the reduction or elimination of weapons. But there are simple things we can do in everyday life that should not be overlooked. Having our own garden where we can cultivate and nurture life is one such vehicle available to all of us. By working a small plot of land with love and care, we can contribute to a more peaceful world. We should not underestimate the power of this simple act. By restoring the balance within nature in a small plot of land—or even one pot—we are doing our part to heal a fractured web of life. The key is there. We just need to take the initiative. This is the message in a seed.

"Respect and love towards the soil brings forth its potential power in yielding crops. The key is to keep the soil free from contamination and to purify it. In response to such attitudes and care, the soil, with a sense of gratitude, will rejuvenate and revitalize itself."

—Meishusama

"THE SEED HAS NO IDEA OF BEING SOME PARTICULAR PLANT, BUT IT HAS ITS OWN FORM AND IS IN PERFECT HARMONY WITH THE GROUND, WITH ITS SURROUNDINGS…AND THERE IS NO TROUBLE. THIS IS WHAT WE MEAN BY NATURALNESS."

—Shrunyu Suzuki
Zen Mind, Beginner's Mind

"FLOWERS AND FRUIT ARE ONLY THE BEGINNING.
IN THE SEED LIES THE LIFE AND THE FUTURE."

—Marion Zimmer Bradley

"THE OLD LAKOTA WAS WISE. HE KNEW THAT
A MAN'S HEART AWAY FROM NATURE BECOMES
HARD; HE KNEW THAT LACK OF RESPECT FOR
GROWING, LIVING THINGS SOON LEADS TO A LACK
OF RESPECT FOR HUMANS TOO."

—Luther Standing Bear

"Soil was made by the Creator in order to produce crops to nourish and sustain humans and animals. Therefore, its essential nature is that of a fertilizer; it is, we could say, no less than a great mass of fertilizer."

—Meishusama

Addendum

Tips for Growing Food in Keeping with Natural Agriculture

For those who would like to practice Natural Agriculture for the first time, we describe its principles, attitude and basic methods in this addendum.

First of all, Shumei Natural Agriculture does not stress specific farming techniques, but rather focuses on the ability to understand and work with the individual conditions of a particular locality. The farmer is guided to understand the farming method that would work best for a particular soil and climate, taking into consideration a vast array of conditions. But there are a few universal guidelines:

The health of the soil and seeds are two essential ingredients for healthy crops. The third essential factor is the mental attitude of the grower. A positive, caring attitude will yield positive results. A skeptical, fearful or doubting attitude will encounter difficulties. Thus, these three factors are the basic conditions of Shumei Natural Agriculture:

1. Pure soil (without fertilizers and agricultural chemicals)

2. Pure seed (home-saved from naturally grown crops)

3. Pure mind (gratitude and a caring attitude toward the soil and crops)

The blend of these three elements, with the addition of light and water, generates the power to grow the highest-quality crops.

Questions often arise about the use of organic fertilizer, as used in organic farming. Natural Agriculture deviates from organic farming in its definition of what can be added to the soil. The Natural Agriculture system developed by

Mokichi Okada does not allow the use of organic fertilizer such as animal manure. It does not add minerals made from natural stone; or charcoal, often used to clean water; or charcoal vinegar or red pepper water, which is sometimes used for pest control. Compost from leftover food or coffee grinds are also not used.

Natural Agriculture does permit the use of natural compost, such as dried grasses and leaves found in the immediate area of the crop cultivation, or compost made of vegetable debris from Natural Agriculture crops. This compost has a purer composition and is used for three important functions:

1. It improves water retention.
2. It helps raise soil temperature.
3. It softens the soil.

Fertilizers, like antibiotics, have the effect of weakening the immune system, so that crops can no longer fight off insects on their own. It takes time for plants to build up resistance, but over several years, the Natural Agriculture farmer will see insects and plant disease decrease significantly. Patience is needed to work with the crops so that they can resist pests through their own natural resources, without the aid of toxic chemicals. The key factors here are patience, commitment to the Natural Agriculture principles, and an attitude of working with nature, not seeking to control or combat it.

Cultivating an attitude of respect and listening to nature will help the farmer navigate through many decisions concerning planting—how deep to sow the seeds, how to till the soil, whether to use raised beds. These are secondary issues, which are easily learned once you begin working in partnership with nature.

Different crops will need varying degrees of sunlight and water, but most need full light and a good amount of moisture. These are key factors to keep in mind when deciding on a location for a vegetable garden. It is also best to select a spot where pesticides and fertilizers have not been used. If there is no alternative, then it is just a matter of time until these chemicals wash out of the soil—it may take a few years, but each year you will see progress as the plants gain strength and build their own internal resistance to pests. If you don't have space for a garden, crops can be grown in planter boxes or wooden boxes. They must be large enough to hold at least 30 centimeters of soil. For good runoff of water, make holes in the bottom of the boxes and cover the bottom with 10 centimers of gravel. This will prevent the roots from getting too wet and rotting.

Each vegetable has its own germination temperature—thus some products are grown in warmer climates. The seeds won't germinate without the needed temperature. Therefore you should consider that the season for sowing seeds differs according to the region and climate. Usually seeds are planted after the danger of frost has passed, but experienced gardeners or farmers in your region can guide you as to the best weeks for planting which crops. The approximate germination temperature for some common crops is as follows:

- Tomato: 20–25 °C
- Lettuce: 15–20 °C
- Cucumber: 20–25 °C
- Eggplant: 25–35 °C
- Cabbage: 15–30 °C
- Squash: 25–28 °C

There are many methods for sowing seeds, depending on the individual farmer. If seeds are planted too deeply, they may not germinate properly because the soil temperature will be too low. In nature, seeds fall to the ground and germinate, without any additional soil being placed over them. We can learn from this and realize that only a little bit of soil is needed. The advantage of covering the seed with soil is that it will keep in the moisture. A good rule of thumb is that the thickness of cover soil should be about twice or three times that of the seed. There is no rule for seed spacing. Plants need some space to keep them from touching and crowding each other.

Trial and error is the best way to develop techniques of cultivation. The important thing is to observe and learn from nature, and to care for your crops so that you are sensitive to their condition and needs.

The time needed for germination varies from vegetable to vegetable. A main concern should be to keep the soil surface from drying out. Planting before a rain is ideal for germination. Otherwise, water the seeds just after they are planted. Regular watering is very important, especially just after planting. If possible, place fallen leaves or dried grass around the roots of the vegetables. This will prevent the soil from drying. This natural compost will enable you to water a little less frequently.

As weeds begin to grow around the crops, plant growth is hampered. Weeds take up water and shade the crops. If the weeds are not over running the crops, weeding is not essential. If they are inhibiting the growth of the crops, it is best to weed. Weeds do play a role in enriching the soil so it is not necessary to rid the soil of all the weeds—just enough so that they don't inhibit plant growth.

As the plants grow, certain techniques will help improve efficiency—such as pruning unnecessary branches, using poles to ensure straight plant growth and using strings to prevent crops like tomatoes from touching the ground. These techniques help guide the natural growing process, rather than control it. By sticking to a few basic principles, the farmer can observe and determine when to step in and aid the plants and when to leave them to their own devices. Plants are living beings and we need only observe, encourage and nurture their life force.

Once the crops are mature, they will yield their own seeds. According to Natural Agriculture, these home-grown seeds from Natural Agriculture crops are the best seeds to use for next year's crop. Each year the ability to harvest seeds will improve, as will the quality of the seeds. The second-year seeds will be better than the first-year seeds. The fifth-year seeds will be better than the second-year seeds, and the tenth-year seeds will be better than the fifth-year seeds. Home-harvested seeds improve with age, and hence future crops will improve in quality. This is one of the secrets of nature.

Some seeds are easier to identify than others. The vegetable plant produces flowers and after the flowers die, fruits are produced. Seeds are produced in the fruits. The seeds of squash are easy to find, while those of lettuce, which are very small and light, are difficult to find. Watch carefully how flowers die and vary. Don't harvest large plants such as tomatoes, eggplant and cucumber too early. Leave them on their branches until they ripen fully, then gather the seeds from them. Dry them on paper and keep them in a bin.

Before you are able to collect your own seeds, and if you cannot find seeds from Shumei Natural Agriculture crops, you can use organic seeds. Never use genetically modified seeds, and you should try not to use F1 seeds, which are seeds developed artificially by biotechnology. They are called hybrid seeds. Though they may be superior to traditional seeds in productivity and uniformity, they don't easily produce seeds, and their seeds when produced are likely to have a different nature. They don't maintain their varieties.

The most important principle to remember in cultivating vegetables is to observe nature and experiment with different cultivation techniques. Nature will guide you, and based on the results, you will learn what works best for your region, climate, soil type and natural setting. Each farmer is a researcher, testing out different methods until nature shows him or her the one that works best for that particular site. Learn to observe, assimilate and respond. Above all, be respectful and caring toward nature.